BOOKWORMS

Shapes!

I See Ovals

Elizabeth Lawrence

Cavendish Square
New York

Published in 2015 by Cavendish Square Publishing, LLC
243 5th Avenue, Suite 136, New York, NY 10016

First Edition

CPSIA Compliance Information: Batch #WW15CSQ

All websites were available and accurate when this book was sent to press.

Library of Congress Cataloging-in-Publication Data

Lawrence, Elizabeth, 1988- author.
I see ovals / Elizabeth Lawrence.
pages cm. — (Shapes!)
Includes index.
ISBN 978-1-50260-264-0 (hardcover) ISBN 978-1-50260-265-7 (paperback) ISBN 978-1-50260-257-2 (ebook)
1. Ovals—Juvenile literature. 2. Shapes—Juvenile literature. 3. Geometry, Plane—Juvenile literature. I. Title.

QA483.L39 2015
516.15—dc23

2014024979

Editor: Kristen Susienka
Copy Editor: Cynthia Roby
Art Director: Jeffrey Talbot
Designer: Douglas Brooks
Senior Production Manager: Jennifer Ryder-Talbot
Production Editor: David McNamara
Photo Researcher: J8 Media

The photographs in this book are used by permission and through the courtesy of:
Cover photo by iStock.com/Image Source; Nick Daly/Getty Images, 5; LazingBee/Getty Images, 7; Tetra Images/Getty Images, 9; Inti St. Clair/Digital Vision/Getty Images, 11; YelenaYemchuk/iStock/Thinkstock, 13; Roman Rybaleov/Shutterstock.com, 15; Paul Bradbury/Caiaimage/Getty Images, 17; Pete Pahham/Shutterstock.com, 19; roberthyrons/iStock/Thinkstock, 21.

Printed in the United States of America

Contents

Oval shapes are all around us.

You find oval shapes in many places.

Some pools have an oval shape.

Have you ever gone to
the beach?

Some beaches have rocks that
are ovals.

Jelly beans are **snacks** shaped like ovals.

They have many colors.

How many colors can you count?

An **avocado** is a **healthy** food.

It is green and shaped like
an oval.

Another food shaped like an oval is an egg.

Some people eat eggs for breakfast.

Some people paint eggs with bright colors in the spring, too.

This mirror is shaped like an oval.

What other things in your house have oval shapes?

Some bathtubs are shaped like ovals.

Bathtubs help us get clean.

They are fun to play in, too.

This girl is wearing glasses.

Her glasses are shaped like ovals.

When you play you see ovals, too!

This train **track** is an oval.

Where else can you find ovals?

New Words

avocado (ah-voh-CA-doh) A dark green vegetable with soft green insides.

healthy (HEL-thee) Something that is good for you.

snacks (SNAKS) Small amounts of food eaten between meals.

track (TRAK) An oval path a toy train or car drives around.

Index

About the Author

Elizabeth Lawrence lives in Albany, New York. She likes to write books, visit new places, and cook.

About BOOKWORMS

Bookworms help independent readers gain reading confidence through high-frequency words, simple sentences, and strong picture/text support. Each book explores a concept that helps children relate what they read to the world they live in.